FRANK MEADOW SUTCLIFFE

Hon F.R.P.S. (1853-1941)

Whitby and its people as seen by one of the founders of the naturalistic movement in photography.

A fourth selection of his work compiled by Michael Shaw.

The Sutcliffe Gallery,
Whitby, North Yorkshire,
England.
Tel: (01947) 602239

First Published 1998
Reprinted 2001
Published and © 2001by:

The Sutcliffe Gallery
1 Flowergate, Whitby, North Yorkshire,
YO21 3BA, England. Tel: (01947) 602239
www.sutcliffe-gallery.co.uk
by agreement with Whitby Literary & Philosophical Society

Photographic printing:	Warrens, Leeds
Photographic finishing:	Colin Roberts, Professional Touch
Scanning & Origination:	Reprotech Studio, York
Artwork:	The House of Type, Guisborough
Duotone printing:	Studio Print, Guisborough
Maritime Research:	Des Sythes
Additional research:	Bill Eglon Shaw
	Tricia Shaw
	Sue Boyes

ISBN Numbers:

Hard Cover Limited Edition:	0 9503175 8 6
Soft Cover General Edition:	0 9503175 9 4

If you would like to order any image in this book as an archival print then please let us have the reference number shown at the end of each caption. Orders can be placed by telephone using a credit card or by cheque, made payable to:- **The Sutcliffe Gallery,** and sent to the address below. If you would like further information on our other products then complete and return the slip to:-

The Sutcliffe Gallery, 1 Flowergate, Whitby, YO21 3BA. Tel. 01947 602239

I would like to order the following archival prints:-

Ref. No/s _____

I enclose my cheque for £ _____

Please charge my Visa/MasterCard/Switch*:

_____

Expiry date:_____   *Issue Number _____

Name: _____
Address: _____
_____
_____
_____
Postcode _____

All of the images in this book are now available as individually produced archival prints. These prints are created using state of the art digital equipment enabling the quality and potential detail in each negative to be fully realised.

They are professionally printed on top quality Archival Matt paper combined with pigmented inks, which give excellent permanence and carry a manufacturers guarantee of 75 years light fastness. * They are printed in sepia (brown) as standard. Black and white prints can be ordered at no extra cost. New technology has opened up this unique collection of photographs to a much wider audience and given Sutcliffe's work a new lease of life.

To order a print quote the reference number at the end of each caption (e.g. 28-12) & complete the reverse of this card.

Two sizes are available:-

210 x 267 mm (8" x 10") @ £20.00

305 x 406 mm (12" x 16") @ £40.00

(The above prices are for **unframed** prints. Delivery approximately 2-3 weeks.
Post & packing charges is £3 per order. For framing details please telephone).

* The Sutcliffe Gallery will replace the print if at any time the superb quality of the image degrades in anyway.

INTRODUCTION

What better time to launch this collection of Sutcliffe's work than 'The Year of Photography' in 1998 which being a European and National event should promote a much greater awareness of photography as an art form.

We will look back on 1998 as being a very important time for us here at The Sutcliffe Gallery as in addition to it being the 'Year of Photography', a further exciting event will have exposed the superb photographs taken by Frank Meadow Sutcliffe to a new and appreciative audience. The Kingston upon Hull Museums and Art Galleries will have mounted a touring exhibition of Sutcliffe's photographs starting at the Ferens Art Gallery in Hull for Easter 1998 and then travelling to venues throughout the Yorkshire region and the rest of the country.

Such is the high quality of Sutcliffe's work that any extra interest in the photographic image created by the above, can only confirm his standing in the history of photography.

To give you a condensed biography on Frank Sutcliffe and to explain how The Sutcliffe Gallery came to be in the very fortunate position of being the sole publishers and copyright holders of this great artist's work, the following brief history may help:

Frank Meadow Sutcliffe was born in Headingley, Leeds in 1853, the son of Thomas Sutcliffe a painter in watercolours whose enthusiasm and encouragement helped Frank in his pursuit of photography. In 1871 Frank's father died, the same year that the Sutcliffe family moved to Whitby. In 1875 after an abortive effort to set up a photographic business in Tunbridge Wells, Sutcliffe returned to Whitby and opened a studio in Waterloo Yard. The following years, when Whitby was increasing in popularity as a holiday resort Sutcliffe would work in his darkroom until late at night after which he went home and continued to mount the photographs he had taken that day. Sutcliffe soon realised that however hard he worked during the short summer season he did not earn enough to carry him through the winter months. Spurred on by financial necessity and a love of photography Sutcliffe began taking photographs in and around Whitby.

His gentle manner and skill in making people feel at ease enabled him to produce photographs which were later to make him internationally famous and win him sixty-two gold, silver and bronze medals.

In 1922 Sutcliffe retired from professional photography and he sold his business, along with his collection of award winning glass plates, to his articled pupil Thomas Waterfall Gillatt.

His retirement lasted for at least one week after which he became the curator of Whitby museum, a position he held until shortly before he died in 1941.

In 1935 The Royal Photographic Society conferred on Sutcliffe their Honorary Fellowship, the highest distinction which can be awarded in the photographic world.

In 1950 Hugh Lambert-Smith bought the business from Gillatt and produced Sutcliffe's photographs up until 1959 when my father, Bill Eglon Shaw, himself a professional photographer, was offered the collection of around 1600 whole plate negatives along with the studio at 1 Flowergate.

Since 1959 we have continued to publish these brilliant photographs by Frank Meadow Sutcliffe, all the time improving the quality of the prints reproduced, hopefully to a standard that would delight Frank Sutcliffe if he were able to see them now.

The Sutcliffe Gallery at 1 Flowergate, established by Bill Eglon Shaw and his wife Dorothy, is now run by Elizabeth their daughter.

When viewing these superb scenes, taken over one hundred years ago, it is so easy to forget what pains and patience had gone into each and every exposure. The brass bound mahogany camera complete with tripod and glass negatives must have weighed heavily on anything but the shortest journey. To form the relaxed poses of the groups of fisher folk we see in this book convinces us that Sutcliffe had a very special talent in directing people.

The undiminished demand for his work from both young and old alike shows that these images of Victorian life are above fad or fashion and hopefully will continue to intrigue and give pleasure to future generations.

From all of us at The Sutcliffe Gallery we hope you enjoy this fourth compilation of photographs by Frank Meadow Sutcliffe.

Michael J. Shaw

'Morning'. An 1870s photograph taken at low water from Dock-End. The barquentine's name cannot be read, but she was a typical work-boat of the period. There were hundreds of these craft working around the coast until they were eventually ousted by the railways from the 1850s onwards, and later by the lorry.   19-11

4

The brig 'Opal' moored alongside where the Endeavour Wharf now stands. The 'Opal' was built at Greenock in 1845, coming to Whitby twenty years later in 1865. She carried a figurehead and a certain amount of decoration around the hawes pipes, which suggests that money was not spared in her building.   B-12

Old Church Street from the corner of the Whitby Bridge about the 1880s. Harker's Jet workshops with the large windows above a coal depot occupy the site of the present slipway. In the background are St. Michael's Church and School, and also the Board School. A paddle steam tug can be seen as well as several small sailing vessels laid up.   C-10

'Herring Season, Whitby'. Dock End with Whitby clinker-built fishing boats. The 84WY can be seen with her nets stowed along the port side. In the background are some Cornish luggers, which were fishing out of the port from the mid 1870s until 1910.   19-49

A fisherman inspects the set of his sail, with some young help on Collier Hope. The coble's sail was a 'dipping lug' which means that on going about on a different tack, the sail had to be lowered, dipped around the mast, and hoisted again on the other side. The lugger in the background was a 'standing lug' which did not have to go through that routine when tacking. Collier Hope was also, as can be seen, a place on which to dry the washing for the folk living on Tate Hill.   16-21

A group of Whitby fishing boats moored off the old steps on New Quay Road.

147BK is a Berwick registered boat, and is drying her nets on a spar rigged between her masts. The foreground boat WY55 was a 'dandy' one of the many ketch-rigged fishing vessels built in the port.   B-26

'Sunshine and Shadow'. This famous Sutcliffe photograph was exhibited internationally and shows the barquentine 'Lively' on the New Quay mooring. An extremely difficult photograph taken against the light where Sutcliffe has cleverly masked the sun behind the sail. Frank Sutcliffe commented:-"Shadow and sun - so our lives are made, yet think how great the sun, how small the shade".   B-42

Marine Parade in the late 1870s. The sailing cobles are moored opposite the Scarborough and Whitby Breweries. Further along the road is the shop with a sun awning, which later became Doran's the Photographers. The building was erected in 1775 as one of the first public subscription libraries in Britain. The large windows were in the reading room, which was also a meeting place for Whitby mariners and shipmasters. 3-57

A misty morning in Whitby lower harbour, with the fishing vessels returning to harbour from a night's fishing. The boat in the foreground is a Whitby 'plosher' (24WY). The rest of the boats are Cornishmen. All of them are being rowed up the harbour either with their own sweeps, or by rowing boats towing them. This was necessary when there was insufficient wind on the ebb tide.   D-16

The 'Welfare', a Hartlepool registered lugger, drying her nets. This had to be done frequently as they were all made from natural fibres. Although they were also regularly 'barked' in a brew made from oak bark, which gave them their distinct colour, they were prone to rot very quickly if stowed away wet. The boats are moored at the New Quay.   17-26

A Paddle Steamer is outward bound after a day trip to Whitby in the 1890s. This particular ship has Scarborough-Grimsby on her stern. Her name would have been on the paddle boxes and therefore cannot be read. Day trips from Bridlington, Filey and Scarborough to Whitby were frequent in Victorian and Edwardian times.   20-47

An 1880s photograph of Whitby Piers, taken forty years before the building of the pier extensions. A high sea is running, with an on-shore wind. Judging by the number of people on the pier end there is probably some incident taking place 'off camera'.   12-31

An unusual photograph, taken with what would now be referred to as a wide angle lens, so that the harbour looks much wider than it actually is. All the children appear to be playing with their model boats, while one man is digging for bait. All the sand on the right-hand side of the photograph has now been dredged away for deeper draught ships and boats.   13-16

An 'against the light' morning photograph of East Whitby, with St. Michael's Church prominent as well as St. Mary's Church and the Abbey house. The brig in the picture is probably laid up with her topgallant masts sent down. This was usual in laid-up ships to reduce windage and weight aloft for lightly ballasted ships.   25-43

The foreground coble is unloading her catch, while the big lugger is drying her nets. The hand-cranked net winch seen aft on the lugger is an interesting forerunner to the powerful haulers used today.   19-44

Scottish 'fifies' in the Dock End circa 1890. The two nearest boats are registered in Kircaldy. Called a 'fifie' after the part of Scotland from which they came, namely, the Kingdom of Fife. With the Cornishmen, they followed the herring around the coast. The foreground cobles are local and show their build of 'three planks to the waterline', and are beautifully maintained.   19-42

The East side beach between Tate Hill Pier and the Fish Pier at Whitby, with washing drying on the beach. The foreground coble seems to have a good number of fish in the bottom, but no evidence of how they were caught as there are no nets or lines visible. It could be that they were being taken across to the East side for kippering. 11-19

'Henry Freeman'. Lifeboatman for over forty years and sole survivor of the Whitby lifeboat disaster of 1861 close by Whitby's West Pier.
The newly introduced Board of Trade cork life jacket Henry Freeman is wearing probably saved his life as the twelve other crew members who
perished, refused to wear such a cumbersome item of attire. 20-23

Jane Fordon giving a 'piggy-back' to Hannah Leadley.
The girls' happy and carefree expressions contrast with the harshness of their environment.   B-48

'Free Education'. Taken on Tate Hill pier, Whitby, with fisherman Robert Leadley giving an al fresco lesson to a bunch of children from the East Side community of which they were all part. His curly haired daughter, Ann, is on the right, sitting on the large wooden chest which would have stored fishing nets.   17-43

'Fisherfolk'. Isobel Batchelor with two fishermen, 'Cud' Colley and Jack Roberts.
Photograph taken by Frank Sutcliffe on Tate Hill Sands in Whitby lower harbour circa 1898. The group is arranged around the fishing coble 'Lily'.   26-50

'Stoking Up'. The crew of a 'mud-hopper' - a primitive type of flat bottomed dredger which was shovelled full of mud at low tide, floated off at high tide and the contents dumped at sea or wherever no obstruction would be caused. The only man identified is Freddie Kingston standing on the left.   20-36

'Four Whitby Fishermen'. From left to right they are: Bill Hawksfield, Jack Fordon, John Batchelor and Ben Weatherill. The wearing of hats was almost universal amongst men at that time (see page 25). An example of Frank Meadow Sutcliffe's genius for natural composition.   4-34

This studio portrait of Mary Ann Middlemass shows the hard-worked hand against her soft young face and gives an insight to the difficult life of the fisher-folk.   20-1

Children playing what is known locally as 'jacks', a game played with a round stone or small ball and five stones. The ball was thrown in the air and the object of the game was to pick up the stones in succession before the ball hit the ground. The group is taken outside David Storry's grocery shop at the foot of the 199 steps which lead up to St. Mary's Parish Church, Whitby.   20-17

'Limpets'. Probably taken around the year 1880, this shows two teenage girls on The Scaur, a bed-rock beach near Whitby's East Cliff. It is clear to see from this photograph why Sutcliffe was recognised as such a fine pictorial photographer.   11-24

'Black and White'. No longer do sweeps become quite so black nor millers quite so white! Bill Batchelor, the sweep, and George Hale of Union Mill, West Cliff, seated on a cart in Flowergate, Whitby, not far from The Sutcliffe Gallery, 1 Flowergate.   B-34

A group photographed in one of Whitby's many yards showing chimney sweep William Batchelor, also shown above in 'Black and White'. The other man, Tom Gains and the girl appear to be repairing a fishing net.   3-99

Thought to be taken along Haggersgate, Whitby. A chimney sweep would have been quite a common site in Victorian times, but of special interest is the young boy, not wearing any form of head gear. This was very unusual although children with bare feet were an everyday sight.   18-22

25

A photograph on Tate Hill Pier. The small boy under the large sou'wester clutches on the sail of his model boat, also being held by 'Stumper' Dryden, so called because of his wooden leg. He lived at 127 Church Street and when he was a boy he fell off Tate Hill pier and lost his leg. 20-42

Two young boys photographed on a seaweed-covered rock at low tide. They are engrossed in collecting shell-fish in a bucket. This carefully arranged genre study once more reinforces Sutcliffe's genius for the sensitive direction of his subjects.   B-20

'Under the Capstan'. Sitting beneath a capstan on the pier at Whitby, are these three young ladies. The two on the left are knitting ganseys, whilst on the right, Elizabeth Colley is crocheting. The girl in the centre is thought to be Mrs Christiana Waller (nee Winspear).   26-7

This photograph depicts a different type of activity taking place on the pier. The man and woman are intent on mending nets beneath the back-drop of St. Mary's Church and Caedmon's Cross.

Note the houses below the church in Henrietta Street, some of which no longer exist due to cliff erosion.   26-29

Cod-a-plenty in barrel and baskets! Sutcliffe entitled this photograph 'The Lost Count' which seems to sum up the overall picture.
This fish market was at Coffee House Corner, circa 1890, only a few yards away from the present fish market.   B-46

Jane Fordon with Hannah Hall holding the basket. These shallow baskets used for collecting bait were also known as 'skiffs' or 'swills'. Photographed on one of the massive rocks strewn on the beach at the foot of Whitby's cliffs.   19-5

A very pleasing composition by Frank Sutcliffe. The first girl leaning into a basket, the second girl knitting, thought to be Christiana Waller (nee Winspear), and both watching the boy mending his toy boat.   3-98

'Boardie Willie'. A sandwich-board man of the 1890s standing against the harbour rail near Whitby's Coffee House Corner. The appeal of this photograph by Sutcliffe lies in its contrived humour.   18-35

'Women in New Way Ghaut, Whitby.' Taken by Frank Sutcliffe during the 1890s in one of the many narrow passages leading down to the harbourside. The edge lighting entering the photograph from the left transforms this from what would have been a rather ordinary figure study to an arresting picture. E-5

33

Two fishermen are cleaning the underside of an up-turned coble on Tate Hill beach, with a little bit of help from two children. In the background the two piers can be seen prior to the building of the extensions in 1912.   11-36

'Mothers Help'. A group of two fisherwomen and two small girls outside a cottage in Whitby. Jane Peart is seated, being helped by her two children.   17-1

'Tom Langlands on Tate Hill Pier, Whitby'. Langlands was born at Seahouses in Northumbria in 1853. At the age of eighteen he became a crew member of Whitby lifeboat and two years later was appointed second coxwain at Upgang (a couple of miles along the coast from Whitby). In 1877, at the age of twenty-four he was made coxwain there.   19-15

'Stern Reality'. Together with the 'Water Rats' this is probably one of Frank Meadow Sutcliffe's best known photographs. The boys are watching boats in the harbour below them. Taken on Scotch Head, Whitby, this photograph was exhibited at the London Camera Club in 1888 and was then entitled 'Excitement'. 24-9

'Gathering Driftwood'. This was only one of the many arduous tasks carried out by fisher-women of the North Yorkshire Coast during the 19th century. This photograph was taken on Whitby Scaur, a beach composed of solid bed-rock. Shipwrecks were commonplace on this coast and provided much of the wood washed ashore. From the left are thought to be, Martha Wood, Elizabeth Ingram, Annie Ingram (Mother), Annie Ingram (Junior) and Jane Fordon.   18-32

'Whitby Fishermen by the Harbour Rail'. Henry Freeman, the sole survivor of Whitby's tragic 1861 lifeboat disaster (third from left) and John Batchelor (sixth from left) are amongst some of the familiar faces which appear on other of Frank Sutcliffe's photographs of Whitby fisherfolk. 17-32

'The Shiplaunch Inn'. Taken along Baxtergate, Whitby, showing what is now 'The Smugglers Cafe'. The archway leads to Loggerheads Yard which takes its name from the ship's loggerhead or figurehead which can be seen to the right of the archway. These premises have changed little in character since this photograph was taken. 3-92

'Church Street, Whitby'. Known as Kirkgate in the 14th century this is the oldest part of the town. Church Street leads from the foot of the 199 steps, the pathway to St. Mary's Parish Church, to Spital Bridge and the Whitehall Ship Yard in the upper harbour. 16-9

Pier Road, Whitby looking towards the Marine Hotel with Marine Parade on the left and Haggersgate to the right. The bridge shown was built in 1835 and was replaced by the present bridge in 1908.   10-20

A fish market attracts a good crowd at Coffee House Corner on Pier Road. The size of the cod laid out on the pavement appear as big as the young boy standing by the barrels observing the lively scene. In this photograph the Marine Hotel has a much smarter appearance when compared to the picture above.   29-46

A view from Baxtergate, Whitby, the buildings on the right of the photograph were once known as 'Boot's Corner' due to Boots the Chemist occupying the premises for many years until they were demolished in the early 1970s. In the background is a boat called the 'Cap Palos', which totally dwarfs the group of three men and dog. The 'Cap Palos' was built in Vancouver in 1919 and was wrecked shortly after, dating this photograph early 1920s.   28-44

Taken from the bridge, looking towards Bridge Street. The Custom House Hotel on the right, now the Dolphin Hotel, is all that remains on the corner site between Grape Lane and the bridge. 28-14

'Whitby Market Place' Taken in 1884 with the Old Town Hall in the background. Rents for the market stalls were collected by John the Bellman, on behalf of the Lord of the Manor and tenants paid from 1s. 6d. to 2s. 0d. per day. In the late 1980s the Market Square was re-cobbled, part of a general refurbishment scheme of the east side of Whitby. 12-11

Looking up Stockton Walk, (now called Brunswick Street) Whitby. The premises for sale on the left have since been demolished. The stationery shop on the right advertises book binding.   19-18

This charming photograph of a little boy in a sailor suit opening the garden gate of 'Park Cottage' is taken on Bagdale, Whitby. This cottage no longer exists and in its place is parkland, part of Pannett Park. A more general view of Bagdale can be seen at the bottom of the next page.   10-48

Sutcliffe has photographed Whitby from this viewpoint on numerous occasions but not often under such clear conditions. Misty and atmospheric scenes of the town are more typical of his work. Taken from an excellent vantage point called 'Spion Kop', also known as 'Burtree Crag'.   8-26

Bagdale Old Hall viewed from Victoria Square on a bleak winter's day. The Hall has 16th century origins but after being converted into tenement flats, needed major restoration in the late 19th century, possibly by the Power family. Further up the road to the right of the picture, the area of the park and Park Cottage can be seen, (shown left).   20-32

Victorian Whitby had its fair share of public houses – as it still does today! Here we have two next door to each other, the Whitby Arms and the Elephant and Castle. Taken along Haggersgate which derived its name from Hagglesygate, an uneven road leading to the sea.   16-35

'Whitby in Winter.' Nowadays it is very rare to see this much snow so near the sea. St. Mary's church is partially masking St. Hilda's Abbey in the misty distance. The summer months would transform this snow-mantled view of Whitby into a bustling seaside resort and busy fishing harbour full of boats. 28-13

'St. Hilda's Abbey, Whitby'. This has been a religious site since 656 A.D. when King Oswy of Northumberland founded St. Hilda's Saxon monastery. The early building was destroyed by Vikings and was re-founded in 1077. Caedmon, the first English poet, lived and worked here as a cowherd. 15-35

'A Bit of News.' Taken by Sutcliffe about 1884, in Cliff Street, Robin Hood's Bay, at this time a tightly knit fishing village. In the photograph, Harrison Alison, reputed to have been the only literate member of the group, is reading to Tommy Baxter, Mary Emerson, who lived at the Almshouses and Lumar William Storm.   24-38

'Bay Bank, Robin Hood's Bay'. Although the muddy road surface has long since been replaced by smooth tarmacadam, the steep gradient still presents difficulties to both pedestrians and motor vehicles. Of interest are the telegraph wires leading down to the centre of the village.   C-12

An unusual view of Robin Hood's Bay. The building on the right of the photograph is the former Congregational church erected in 1840. It was re-named the United Reformed Church in 1972 after the union of Presbyterian and some Congregational churches.   18-10

'Toy Boats'. Compositionally this photograph breaks most of the rules – certainly those by which 19th century photography was ordered –
yet the result is as satisfying as one could wish for. The setting is at Runswick Bay, a few miles along the coast to the north-east of Whitby,
at that time a small fishing village. 2-60

Runswick Bay photographed from the beach with the Lifeboat house in the centre. The first lifeboat stationed in Runswick was called 'The Sheffield', later replaced by the 'Margaret and Edward'. The white house on the cliff is 'The Royal Hotel'.   5-30

Washing laid out to dry on bushes at Runswick Bay. It would have been a common sight in the late 1800s for laundry to be dried in a communal area such as this. The double gabled house to the right is named 'Prospect House' and advertises refreshments. Nearby, to the left is a very small thatched cottage.   12-6

View of Staithes with Cowbar Bridge in the mid-distance. The iron railway bridge in the background was part of the Whitby to Stockton line and was demolished in the 1950s. A common sight in Victorian times, maybe, but a bit more unusual now is the large number of hens strutting around the banks of Cowbar Beck.   12-29

'The Young Orthographer and his Grandfather'. Taken at Staithes around 1890 this photograph shows a young boy pointing out the mis-spelling of 'Campbell' on the bow of the beached coble.   24-22

An unusual view of Sandsend with Whitby in the distance. The lengths of timber on the left would have been from the Mulgrave Estate and even today there is a timber yard in Mulgrave Woods just off to the right of this photograph.   9-6

A picturesque village scene of a footbridge over Sandsend Beck. The Church and the row of cottages to the left are still there today. Sandsend has become a very popular village with holiday-makers, full of character and charm, offering the sand and sea together with rural settings as in this photograph.   9-12

'Milk Maid'. A beautiful rural study of Lorna McNeil of Longstone Farm, Low Hawsker, taken about 1902. The McNeil family later emigrated to White Rock, Canada where she lived until her death in 1984. 14-9

Another fine rural study, this time of Mrs Ann Scarth of Rock Head Cottage, Glaisdale and her brother-in-law George Scarth. George and his brother Isaac made besoms (brooms or sweeping brushes) and large woven baskets, known locally as 'scuttles'.   B-22

'Scally Bank, Egton'. Taken by Frank Sutcliffe in 1881, this carefully arranged photograph shows an Egton Estate wagon drawn by a team of four horses, ascending the steep hill from Egton Bridge to Goathland. 11-23

A restful rural scene on the riverbank at Egton Bridge. The large house in the background, 'Bridgeholme', used to be the Egton Estate offices until the early 1950s when they moved closer to 'Egton Manor'. The river in this photograph, the 'Esk', is not long at 24 miles, but is now Yorkshire's only salmon river. C-1

'Catching Newts'. Two of Sutcliffe's children, Horace and Irene, fishing for newts. The pond is probably at Hart Hall Farm, Glaisdale, a village on the side of the Esk Valley approximately ten miles from Whitby. A-47

'Barn Door Fowls'. Taken at Lealholm Hall Farm, a popular location for Sutcliffe's rural photographs. During the summer months the Sutcliffe family rented a cottage in Glaisdale, a couple of miles from Lealholm. Whilst they were in residence Frank travelled daily by train to his portrait studio in Whitby.   D-11

'The Ingathering'. Taken around 1895 at Four Lane Ends Farm, Whitby. At one time a tollgate was part of the farm through which Bonnie Prince Charlie is reputed to have passed one stormy night. One of Frank Meadow Sutcliffe's finest rural compositions.   24-16

A farm scene, possibly taken at Sleights, a sizeable village approximately four miles from Whitby. Frank Sutcliffe had a rare talent of being able to create a pleasing picture from a situation most photographers would pass by.   7-16

'Among the Turnips'. One of Sutcliffe's fine rural studies demonstrating his mastery of the whole plate camera. He is believed to have titled this photograph "Man goeth forth to his labour until the evening". Over the years the less poetic but more simple title has been adopted. 16-39

Sleights main street with two timber carts approaching the camera, whilst three young boys look on as a horse-drawn sledge makes its way up the slight incline. Some movement is evident in the horses' heads, but this does not in any way detract from the charm of this picture. 19-1

A farmer unloading a cart of manure. This photograph, most likely taken around Lealholm, is unusual in that both foreground and background are out of focus, demonstrating a very limited depth of field. The short exposure time necessary to 'freeze' the farmer's actions would have dictated a relatively large aperture, thus producing the minimal depth of focus seen here.   25-33

A team of three horses pulling a cart-load of straw into the farmyard, probably at Lealholm Hall. The pond in the foreground would have been used to soak or 'steep' the straw to prepare it for thatching. 'Steeping' the straw made it softer to work with when being used to thatch stacks of hay to protect them from the elements.   25-36

Taken at Hurricane Corner, at the top of Lealholm Bank. The sheep are grazing as the early morning sun starts to burn away the mist. Yet another photograph by Frank Meadow Sutcliffe demonstrating his mastery of using sunlight and mist to transform an everyday scene into a work of art. 4-26

'Winter at Glen Esk'. The road from Ruswarp, a small village just outside Whitby, crosses Stainsacre Beck by the little hump-backed bridge before winding steeply up the hill known as 'Danger Bank'. In his book 'Whitby Lore and Legend', published in 1923, Percy Shaw Jeffrey writes: "Cockmill, in Glen Esk, was a great rendezvous for smugglers who had their stow holes in the surrounding woods". D-47

'Trees in a Misty Valley'. A composition which under almost any other lighting and atmospheric conditions would be mundane, becomes a thing of beauty under the influence of 'sea fret' – a costal fog frequently experienced on the North Sea coast. This photograph by Frank Meadow Sutcliffe gained an award at a Tokyo exhibition in 1893. 4-17